LIFE Ronald Reagan

A LIFE IN PICTURES

6 Foreword

8 # An American Boy

18 Sporting Presidents

20 # Hollywood Bound

46 Presidents in the Movies

48 # A Time of Transition

58 The Great Communicators

60 # Governor Reagan

74 Prominent First Ladies

76 # President Reagan

118 Assassinations

120 # The Legacy

PETE SOUZA/THE WHITE HOUSE

LIFE Ronald Reagan

A LIFE IN PICTURES

By Robert Sullivan
and the Editors of LIFE

With a Foreword by Dan Rather

LIFE Ronald Reagan

A LIFE IN PICTURES

Editor Robert Andreas

Picture Editor Barbara Baker Burrows

Art Director Ian Denning

Writer Robert Sullivan

Reporters Hildegard Anderson, Lela Nargi, Deirdre Van Dyk

Associate Picture Editor Christina Lieberman

Picture Research Lauren Steel

Copy Chief Kathleen Berger

Copy Desk Cheryl Brown, Madeleine Edmondson, Joel Griffiths, Larry Nesbitt, Pam Warren

LIFE Books

Time Inc. Home Entertainment

President
Stuart Hotchkiss

Executive Director, Branded Businesses
David Arfine

Executive Director, Non Branded Businesses
Alicia Longobardo

Executive Director, Time Inc. Brand Licensing
Risa Turken

Director, Licensing
Scott Rosenzweig

Executive Director, Marketing Services
Carol Pittard

Director, Retail & Special Sales
Tom Mifsud

Director, Branded Businesses
Maarten Terry

Associate Directors
Roberta Harris
Kenneth Maehlum

Product Managers
Dana Gregory
Andre Okolowitz
Ann Marie Ross
Niki Viswanathan
Daria Raehse

Associate Product Managers
Victoria Alfonso
Jennifer Dowell
Dennis Sheehan
Meredith Shelley
Lauren Zaslansky

Assistant Product Managers
Ann Gillespie
Meredith Peters
Virginia Valdes

Telemarketing Manager
Marina Weinstein

Associate Manager, e-Commerce
Dima Masrizada

Licensing Manager
Joanna West

Associate Licensing Manager
Regina Feiler

Licensing Coordinator
Laury Shapiro

Associate Manager, Retail & New Markets
Bozena Szwagulinski

Coordinator, Retail Marketing
Gina Di Meglio

Editorial Operations Director
John Calvano

Assistant Editorial Operations Manager
Emily Rabin

Book Production Manager
Jessica McGrath

Associate Book Production Manager
Jonathan Polsky

Assistant Book Production Manager
Suzanne DeBenedetto

Fulfillment Manager
Richard Perez

Assistant Fulfillment Manager
Tara Schimming

Financial Director
Tricia Griffin

Financial Manager
Robert Dente

Associate Financial Manager
Steven Sandonato

Assistant Financial Manager
Tamara Whittier

Executive Assistant
Mary Jane Rigoroso

Copyright 2000
Time Inc. Home Entertainment
ISBN: 1-929049-05-6
Library of Congress Catalog Number:
00-101244

We welcome your comments and suggestions about LIFE Books.
Please write to us at:
LIFE Books
Attention: Book Editors
PO Box 11016
Des Moines, IA
50336-1016

If you would like to order any of our Hard Cover Collector's Edition books, please call us at
1-800-327-6388
(Monday through Friday, 7:00 a.m.–8:00 p.m. or Saturday, 7:00 a.m.–6:00 p.m. Central Time).

LIAISON AGENCY

Foreword

BY DAN RATHER

In 1994, the world learned that Ronald Wilson Reagan was suffering from Alzheimer's disease. The news came from a brief letter, written in Reagan's own hand on stationery bearing the presidential seal and dated November 5, 1994—14 years and one day after an electoral landslide made him the 40th President of the United States. "I now begin," the letter read, "the journey that will lead me into the sunset of my life."

He has been called the Great Communicator, and his signature cadence and mellifluous rasp have ridden the American airwaves for the better part of 70 years now. In the years since Reagan embarked on that final journey, we have heard his voice only from fading bits of video, pieces of a recent past rendered so very distant by the breathtaking pace of change at century's end and century's dawn. But once that voice spoke to America directly. From the small screen and the big screen and the wireless, in the career of an actor, a corporate spokesman, a sports announcer. It spoke from the California governor's mansion and it spoke from the White House, where Reagan's eloquence in framing the American moment stands as perhaps his greatest legacy.

It is, of course, too soon for us to know how history will judge the Reagan presidency; the battle to define its legacy, and his, roils still. To the partisans of the "Reagan Revolution," his is a face that would benefit and befit Mount Rushmore; to their opposites, the Reagan White House stands at the center of a decade that memory has rendered synonymous with rapaciousness and greed. Some point first to the legislative triumphs of his first term; others to the foreign-policy malfeasance of his second. The divide is evident in how one views America's current run of economic good fortune. To some, this is the Clinton boom. To others, it is simply and self-evidently the Reagan expansion, 18 years of growth interrupted only by the brief recession of 1991.

Reagan's was the last presidency to fight the cold war from beginning to end, and there are those who credit him with winning it. Honest observers on both sides can debate over whether victory, such as it is, was the fruit of 40 years of bipartisan continuity in American foreign policy or the Reagan will to stand up to and outspend the Soviet Union wherever and whenever necessary. But however one comes down on that question, it was undeniably Ronald Reagan who had the best lines before the iron curtain came down. It was he who stood at Berlin's Brandenburg Gate in 1987, and facing East Germany and the "evil empire" beyond, intoned, "Mr. Gorbachev, tear down this Wall." Two years later, words became deed.

Whether Ronald Reagan drove the tide of history or was carried on the crest of its breaking wave is not a judgment that we can properly make. That falls to those who will come after us, long after the partisans and the detractors and the man himself have ridden into that final sunset. Posterity has so often shown us a middle view between the pressing debates of an era, and has a way of illuminating features we cannot see now with the light of a future we cannot know.

But we can recount what we know. The Reagan presidency began on the front steps of the Capitol, the inaugural ceremony facing west toward the Mall and its monuments for the first time in history. In that first inaugural address, Reagan sounded the themes he had campaigned on and would return to and repeat throughout his presidency—the need, as he saw it, to cut federal spending and the reach of big government, his hope for peace through strength and, what may be most important of all, his call to "realize that we're too great a nation to limit ourselves to small dreams."

This plea to "begin an era of national renewal" was the essence of Reagan's popular and populist appeal, as was his almost incantatory repetition of the three words that gave birth and definition to the American experiment: "We the People." We the People moved through the text of his inaugural oratory, and We were invoked in his farewell address, eight years later. He tried so often to remind us that, from We the People—not, need it be said, government—would come the solutions to our greatest problems.

He asked a nation to find within itself the greatness that he considered its birthright, and he sought to make us equal to the task by reminding us of our collective heritage. Reagan was the Great Communicator, yes, but he was also a master at communicating greatness. He understood that, as he once put it, "History is a ribbon always unfurling" and managed to convey his vision in terms both simple and poetic. From his first inaugural, as he looked west past the Mall to Arlington National Cemetery:

"Each one of those markers is a monument to the kind of hero I spoke of earlier. Their lives ended in places called Belleau Wood, the Argonne, Omaha Beach, Salerno and halfway around the world on Guadalcanal, Tarawa, Pork Chop Hill, the Chosin Reservoir, and in a hundred rice paddies and jungles of a place called Vietnam."

Then, in a trademark touch, the easy move from the grand tableau to the concrete, the personal example and exemplar:

"Under one such marker lies a young man, Martin Treptow,* who left his job in a small town barbershop in 1917 to go to France with the famed Rainbow Division. There, on the western front, he was killed trying to carry a message between battalions under heavy artillery fire.

"We're told that on his body was found a diary. On the flyleaf under the heading, 'My Pledge,' he had written these words: 'America must win this war. Therefore I will work, I will save, I will sacrifice, I will endure, I will fight cheerfully and do my utmost, as if the issue of the whole struggle depended on me alone.'"

Finally, the coup de grâce, connecting past with present: *"The crisis we are facing today does not require of us the kind of sacrifice that Martin Treptow and so many thousands of others were called upon to make. It does require, however, our best effort . . ."*

One senses that, for Reagan, the ghosts of history were entirely visible. One can imagine that when he, as was his habit, contemplated the vista from his favorite White House window, he could see the faraway smoke rising from the Battle of Bull Run, as he was told Lincoln had before him. That he addressed Con-

---

*Ed.: Treptow was actually buried in Bloomer, Wis. Reagan's speechwriters accepted the blame for the error.

gress in halls that still echoed with the voices of Webster and Clay.

Much has been made of Ronald Reagan's sentimentality, his sepia-toned vision of a Norman Rockwell past. But one is struck, looking back over what he said during eight years in the White House, with how often he used the past to illuminate the present and the future. I am not the first to call attention to this; the biographer Edmund Morris goes so far as to suggest that Reagan had little use for nostalgia in and of itself.

For Ronald Reagan, the distinctions of past, present, future, may have been irrelevant. He remained a constant in the eight years he occupied 1600 Pennsylvania Avenue, his outlook, if not always his deeds, unwavering from first word to last. And so he was able to act as a conduit to connect us to who we had been and who we could be.

His letter of November 5, 1994, poignant yet devoid of self-pity, tells us he is once again looking west. But Ronald Wilson Reagan also could not resist one more look back over his shoulder. He makes his ride confident in his knowledge that, as he wrote, "for America there will always be a bright dawn ahead."

May we all share his optimism. And may his steed hold steady as he completes his journey.

An American Boy

In the mid-1960s, Ronald Reagan, a Hollywood actor who was recasting himself as a national politician, paused to reminisce about his boyhood. He recalled gaslit streets in small Illinois towns. He talked of adventures in the woods and at treacherous swimming holes, of an existence that was "one of those rare Huck Finn–Tom Sawyer idylls." He remembered being perched on his older brother's secondhand bike, "hanging onto a hitching post in front of the house," waiting for his dad. "I was always there at noon when he came home for lunch. He would push me around in the street for a few exhilarating circles." He recalled his loving mother teaching him to read before he was five. He recounted bygone pickup football games. "The lure of sweat and action always pulled me back to the game—despite the fact that I was a scrawny, undersized, underweight nuisance," he said. "As a result, I had a collection of the largest purplish-black bruises possible. More than once, I must have been a walking coagulation. Those were the happiest times of my life."

Reagan painted lovely sepia-toned pictures of his youth. The images were charming to his audience. And were they true?

A skinny, scrappy boy who would become a strapping man, Ronald Reagan played right guard on the football team at Dixon (Ill.) High, where he also participated in basketball and track. His family was poor, and summertime meant work as well as play: caddying, laboring on a construction crew, eventually lifeguarding.

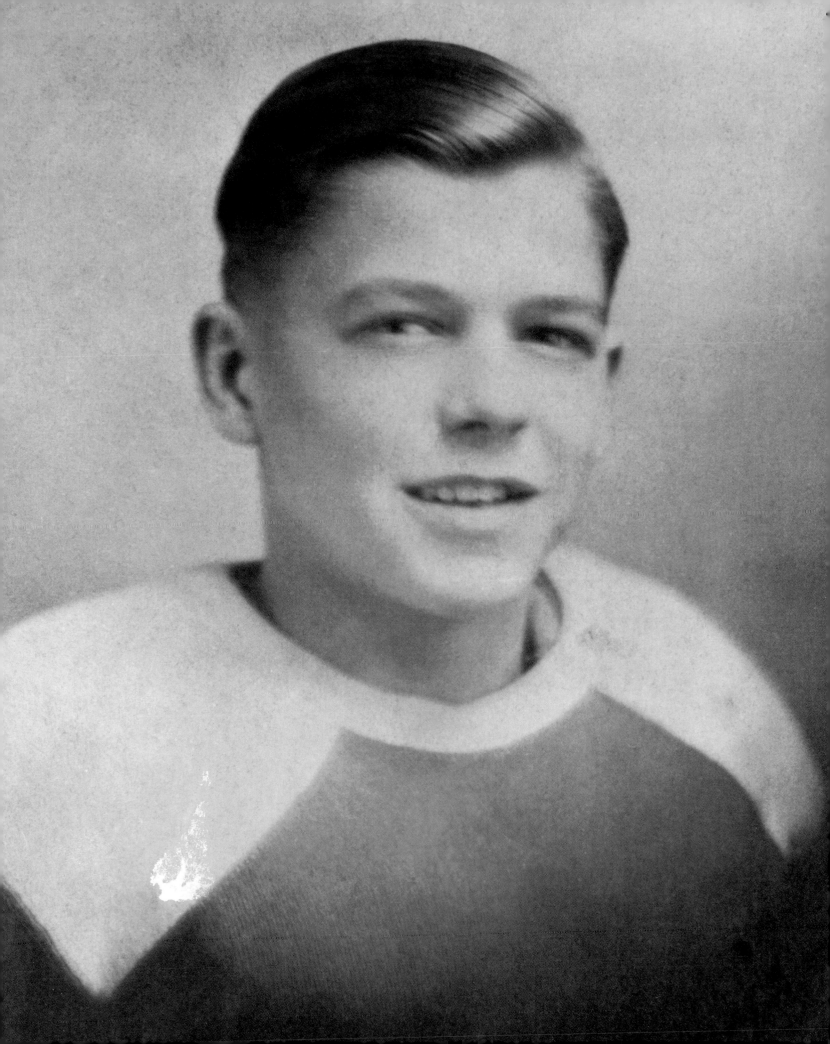

On February 6, 1911, Jack Reagan heard his newborn's cry and said, "For such a little bit of a fat Dutchman, he makes a hell of a lot of noise."

"I think he's perfectly wonderful," said Jack's wife, Nelle.

The baby was not a Dutchman but the son of a first-generation Irish Catholic father and a Scotch Protestant mother—yet the nickname, Dutch, would stick his entire life. Ronald Wilson "Dutch" Reagan, the younger of two boys, was born in the country town of Tampico, Ill., to a shoe salesman and his wife. The family moved regularly from one rented home to another, and by the time Dutch was nine he had lived in several small towns and on Chicago's South Side. There were, to be sure, many fine adventures with his brother, Neil, but there was darkness as well. Jack Reagan, as tall and strong a man as Dutch would grow to be, was seriously addicted to alcohol. He went on week-long benders and suffered from blackouts. In a 1965 memoir, *Where's the Rest of Me?*, Ronald Reagan recalled his "first moment of accepting responsibility." A boy of 11, he had returned to the family's home in Dixon to find his father on the front porch, "spread out as if he were crucified—as indeed he was—his hair soaked with melting snow, snoring as he breathed." Dutch had, theretofore, been shielded from his father's problem by Neil and Nelle—though of course he heard the shouting in the night. His instinct this time was to pretend his dad wasn't there, to walk over him and scurry to his bedroom. But no one else was there to deal with the situation, so the boy grabbed his father's overcoat, dragged him inside and got him to bed. "In a few days he was the bluff, hearty man I knew and loved and will always remember."

This postscript was characteristic. Throughout Ronald Reagan's life he

MPTV

would be the optimist: He would seize upon better memories, he would seek—and find—silver linings. This aspect of his personality was immensely appealing, and while Dutch Reagan was famous as a loner with few intimate friends, he was also, from the first, charismatic and extremely popular.

Jack Reagan held strong political convictions. He was "a sentimental Democrat, who believed fervently in the rights of the workingman," Ronald recalled. A staunch Roman Catholic in an era when Catholics were second-class citizens, Jack preached tolerance in his household. Family lore maintained that he refused to let the kids see D.W. Griffith's *The Birth of a Nation* at the local movie house because it condoned racial bigotry, and that once, on a sales call, he slept a cold night in his car rather than stay at a hotel that barred Jews. Whatever the truth of these anecdotes, Dutch got from his father a passion for political thought and a belief that the Democratic party was the people's protector. The former, at least, would last a lifetime.

Despite his father's influence, Ronald

The future President spent his formative years primarily in rural towns in Illinois. At the age of eight, a pensive Dutch posed with his Tampico elementary school classmates. By the time he was entering his teens (opposite), the Reagan family had moved to Dixon, where his father became part owner of a shoe store.

DONALD REAGAN
"Dutch"

"Life is just one grand sweet song, so start the music."

Pres. N. S. Student Body 4; Pres. 2; Play 3, 4; Dram. Club 3, 4, Pres. 4; Fresh.-Soph. Drama Club 1, 2, Pres. 2; Football 3, 4; Annual Staff; Hi-Y 3, 4, Vice-Pres. 4; Art. 1, 2; Lit. Contest 2; Track 2, 3.

He was never named Donald; the editor of the high school yearbook simply messed up. As is evident from the activities listed here, Dutch was hardly anonymous on campus—he had, in fact, secured several of his first presidencies.

was very much his mother's son. Neil had been baptized a Catholic, but Ron was raised in Nelle's Disciples of Christ Church. She was an evangelist and something of a missionary, caring for the sick, visiting prisoners, giving talks, at one point even writing a play for her church in Dixon. (The Disciples of Christ supported temperance—Carry Nation was a member—and in Nelle's play a young girl says to her father, "I love you, Daddy, except when you have that old bottle.") Young Ronald worked after school at the church and acted in some of those church plays. He heard his mother's talks, and years later said that his own early speeches had been modeled on hers. Ronald Reagan inherited his mother's propensity for seeing only the good in people, as well as his mother's firm belief that God's will was at work in all things.

If mother and son were correct about this, then God did a fine job in landing Dutch at Dixon's Lowell Park. There, in 1926, he began working as a lifeguard on the Rock River for $15 a week. During the next seven summers he saved the lives of no fewer than 77 people; it is difficult to corroborate many of the tales from Reagan's early years, but by all accounts he did rescue 77 swimmers. This young man who would, in the years to come, continually float between real and illuso-

In a high school drama, Dutch played opposite his girlfriend, Margaret "Mugs" Cleaver. He followed her to college, but the relationship fizzled when, on a trip abroad, she fell in love with an attorney whom she would marry. Dixon High's yearbook says that Dutch, second from left, "took care of his tackle berth in a creditable manner, and certainly had the true 'Dixon Spirit.'"

Scrawny no longer, Dutch saved 77 lives as a lifeguard—and carved a notch into a log for each one. At Eureka College he played varsity football for three years, starred in swimming, served as president of the Boosters Club and the student senate, wrote for the school paper and was a features editor of the yearbook. And: "I copped the lead in most plays."

ry images of all-American champions was, in his late teens and early twenties, a bona fide American hero.

He graduated from Dixon High in 1928, a fair student, a fine athlete and already a leader (he was student body president). In the fall he matriculated at Eureka (Ill.) College, a religious school. He supplemented his scholarship money by washing dishes at his TKE fraternity house, meanwhile continuing his so so academic career and his ever more vibrant public life. "I loved three things: drama, politics and sports," he later remembered. "And I'm not sure they always came in that order." He won letters in football and swimming, joined the drama club, worked on the college newspaper and became involved in school politics. When students called for the resignation of Eureka's president, they asked Reagan to speak on the issue in chapel. His rousing speech drew a roar and helped spur the students to go on strike. "That audience and I were together," Reagan said. He realized that he was a man who could connect with, and inspire, the people.

Back home, things weren't getting easier. In the midst of the Depression, Jack Reagan lost his shoe store. In the fall of 1932 he and his son Ronald voted for Franklin Delano Roosevelt for President.

REAGAN

Sporting Presidents

Ronald Reagan was a swimmer and footballer. Other Chief Executives also learned valuable lessons on the playing fields of America.

William Taft, Golfer
A very big golfer, he was also a baseball fan. In 1910 he became the first President to open the Major League season with a ceremonial toss.

George Bush, Baseball Player
As President he could play a round of golf in two hours. At Yale he hit .264 as captain of a championship team.

Theodore Roosevelt, Boxer
The Rough Rider was a marksman, a hunter, a tennis player and, during his days at Harvard (above), a boxer. Kinsman F.D. Roosevelt loved to swim.

George Washington, Horseman
He not only rode in war, he also rode for recreation; on occasion he rode to hounds (above).

18

John F. Kennedy, Sailor
A deft hand at the tiller, he was quietly the best golfer among the Presidents; he played down his talent for this Republican game.

Gerald Ford, Football Player
Perhaps the finest athlete ever to reside at 1600 Pennsylvania Avenue, Ford received offers to play pro football after his MVP senior season at Michigan.

Dwight D. Eisenhower, Fisherman
Ike, famous as a golfer, had a putting green outside the Oval Office. The old general was also an avid fisherman.

Richard Nixon, Bowler
He bowled in the Executive Office Building (above) and had a lane installed at the White House. A foot note: Did the President's men tell him when he stepped over the line?

Hollywood Bound

The scene is a midwestern city—Des Moines—during the Great Depression. It is evening. A bus pulls in and a young woman gets off. She sets off down the street. A man follows her. Suddenly, he is on her. She feels a gun in her back, and he tells her to drop the purse and suitcase. She has only three dollars and offers that. The man grabs the purse and suitcase. Then, the hero appears in an apartment window two floors above the street. "Leave her alone," he shouts, "or I'll shoot you right between the shoulders." The mugger drops everything and flees. The hero descends the stairs and comforts the lady in distress.

The hero was played by Ronald Reagan. The woman was Melba Lohmann, playing herself. The year was 1933 and the scene was real. Reagan may or may not have had a gun; if he had one, it may or may not have been loaded. Through the years, even his accounts of the story differed. But the significant point is: Ronald Reagan could be the hero, on screen or in life. He could play it to people's satisfaction. If he embroidered, no one much cared. His audience was taken with the performance, and felt that behind it was a man they could trust.

Reagan radiated midwestern strength and exuberance in this 1942 Warner Bros. publicity still. Coming off a stellar performance in *Kings Row*, he was at the apex of his film career, but military service would limit him to just one movie from 1943 through '46.

MPTV

Dutch Reagan loved Eureka College, a school of 250 students founded by the Disciples of Christ, and he loved Margaret "Mugs" Cleaver, a former classmate from Dixon High who, during their final months together at Eureka, became his fiancée. In college, Dutch was distanced from—if not immune to—the country's economic misery and the struggles of the Reagans back in Dixon. He moved from glory to glory, growing stronger and more successful as an athlete, feeling the joy of a man in love, drinking the "heady wine" of being a leader.

In 1932, only 7 percent of Americans were in college, while 12 million of them—25 percent of the adult population—were out of work. That was the year Dutch graduated into the world.

He already knew he would play a large part in the survival of his family. It was he who had helped persuade his older brother, Neil, a.k.a. Moon, to join him at Eureka and improve his lot. It was he who had the best summer jobs and was able to contribute to the family pot. Now it was he who analyzed the situation and decided to be an entertainer—a Depression-proof profession. In 1932 radio was hot, so Dutch set his sights on radio.

WHO was a 50,000-watt radio station, and Dutch Reagan reached an audience beyond the Midwest with his baseball re-creations. By 1937 he had signed with Warner Bros. In those days, a studio often broke its film stars in gradually, and in Reagan's first three films, he barely had to act. He played a radio announcer, a radio announcer and (opposite, in *Swing Your Lady*) a sports reporter.

Chicago didn't want him, but Davenport, Iowa, took him. Dutch Reagan, sportscaster and announcer, went on the air at WOC (World of Chiropractic, believe it or not) in February 1933. A portion of his $100 per month—an enormous sum in that place and time—was mailed home to Dixon, where his father was unemployed.

Dutch quickly got himself fired when he failed to mention a program sponsor. WOC could not find an immediate replacement, and Reagan was still hanging around the studio, doing occasional temporary on-air work, when he was sent in the spring to work at WHO, a sister station in Des Moines. This much-larger NBC affiliate rehired Reagan as a full-time employee.

Davenport was 75 miles from Dixon, but Des Moines was 250 miles west—

In his first film, *Love Is On the Air* (1937, above), Reagan blurred fact and fiction to a delicious degree, playing a wide-eyed smalltown radio announcer. In 1939's *Dark Victory* (right) he played violently against type as a rich, bleary-eyed roué with designs on Bette Davis (who responded much as she did in real life). Reagan found his own performance wanting.

Jane Wyman and Reagan clicked in 1938 in *Brother Rat*, then accompanied Louella Parsons on her 1939 vaudeville tour. The gossip columnist, who was from Dixon, hosted a wedding reception for the couple at her home on January 26, 1940.

a world away. And Reagan's world changed. The girl he left behind, Mugs Cleaver, met a man on her European tour and broke off her engagement to Dutch. Reagan would write in his memoirs: "As our lives traveled into diverging paths . . . our lovely and wholesome relationship did not survive growing up." Also in Des Moines, Reagan got his first taste of professional success and celebrity—even a kind of stardom. His rise as a sportscaster on one of the most far-reaching radio stations in the Midwest brought him a threefold raise to $75 a week. He bought a Nash convertible, nice clothes—and still had money to send home.

It was the era of baseball re-creations, and Reagan had a distinct flair for taking black-and-white information and making it colorful. He would receive updates via telegraphy from the ballpark and would

"We do the same foolish things that other couples do, have the same scraps, about as much fun," said Reagan in a 1941 press release. "The Reagans' home life is probably just like yours, or yours, or yours." Except for the pool, of course.

PHOTOFEST

MOVIE STILL ARCHIVES

bring them to life for his listeners with all the appropriate bells and whistles: the crack of the bat, the roar of the crowd. He broadcast 600 games over four years and became not only a source of news but of reliability for millions. Hugh Sidey, who many years later would cover Reagan as a *Time* magazine editor, was a boy in Dust Bowl Iowa in the 1930s, and once mused that Reagan, calling a baseball game, always gave him the feeling that life was going to get better.

Dutch Reagan, now a well-known broadcaster enjoying his celebrity, was, in 1937, ready to attempt a big leap. The Chicago Cubs' spring training camp was

A star is born: Two of Reagan's early films, *Knute Rockne* (above) and *King's Row* (right), made him a household name. Although he would never be known as an actor whose skills approached those of costars Pat O'Brien or Ann Sheridan, he turned in fine performances in the films—two of his favorites.

Warners' publicity stills portrayed a wholesome, happy, smiling Reagan (opposite). It helped that the image matched the man, but in any event, to adoring fans, the image *was* the man (above). Part of Reagan's appeal was that he was safe at a time when America needed to feel safe. He was not marketed as a playboy but as a good guy and loyal husband—and that took no role-playing.

on Catalina Island off the California coast, and Reagan coaxed WHO into sending him to Hollywood to file reports. He then had a friend of a friend set up a screen test at Warner Bros., and after filling in blanks that transformed Eureka College's drama club into some kind of semipro theatrical troupe, he showed up for an interview with agent Bill Meiklejohn. "I have another Robert Taylor sitting in my office," Meiklejohn told Warners' casting director Max Arnow, who agreed for the most part with the assessment. Reagan was told to ditch the "Dutch" nickname, lose the eyeglasses—and report for work in June, at $200 a week. Adieu, Des Moines.

Like other Hollywood male actors, Reagan was handsome, preternaturally photogenic and well-spoken. Unlike some of them, he was not a naturally gifted actor and frequently came across as one-dimensional. But, rare among them, he was sober-minded and willing to work as hard as he had to for success. On his first day on the set he had trouble reading the script because of his bad eyes (he had worn horn-rims since he was 13). He struggled through the day, then resolved to memorize all his lines before showing up each morning—something he would do throughout his career.

The film *Brother Rat* (1938) is significant for two reasons: It marked Reagan's

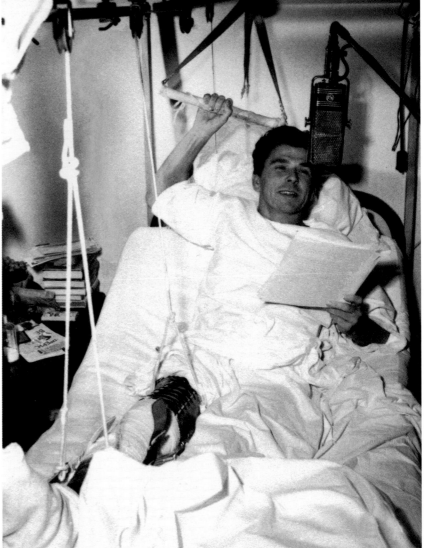

In 1940, University of Southern California art students chose the 6'1", 180-lb. Reagan—32" waist, 41" chest—as their "20th Century Adonis," he of the perfect physique. Reagan said thanks by posing for a sculpture class. In real life, no one's perfect: Reagan was hospitalized with pneumonia in 1947, and in 1949 (above) was laid up after breaking his leg in six places playing baseball.

first big popular success, and on that production he met the actress Jane Wyman, whom he would marry in January 1940. That year—1940—turned out to be a very good one for Reagan, as his portrayal of the doomed Notre Dame running back George Gipp in the film *Knute Rockne—All American* represented a critical breakthrough. Reagan was well-suited to capture Gipp's athleticism and his brave stoicism in confronting a fatal illness. The actor knew it, lobbying hard for the role. Other performers, he said later, "could have played the part better, but no one could have wanted to play it more than I did." And no one could have foreseen how useful an association with

Gipp—not to mention the rallying cry "Win one for the Gipper!"—might be in a later career.

Slogans from Reagan's early movies became part of who he was and who he would become. In *Kings Row* (1942) he gave perhaps his finest performance, as a playboy whose legs are needlessly amputated. When he awakens after surgery, the character looks down and cries out, "Where's the rest of me?"—a question Reagan would challenge himself with in the years to come, and also the title of candidate Reagan's 1965 memoir.

"THE HOPEFUL REAGANS," declared the press release. **"They Are Looking Forward to More of Everything Good—Including Children." Maureen, above, was born in 1941, and Michael was adopted in 1945. But everything else was not, in fact, good—and one afternoon Wyman simply told Reagan to "get out." As she put it in her succinct courtroom statement suing for divorce: "There was nothing in common between us, nothing to sustain our marriage."**

Left and above: At his ranch in Northridge, Dutch always loved horses and was an excellent rider. In more than one movie, he refused to yield the saddle to a stunt double, and he often executed his own jumps. His three California retreats, with their combination of sun and trails, would over the years be sources of revivification for Reagan.

In wartime Hollywood, Reagan was something of an odd duck. Having enlisted in the 14th Cavalry Regiment of the U.S. Army Reserve in 1937, he was called up after Pearl Harbor. While he certainly appeared 1A, his poor eyesight kept him from combat, and eventually he was assigned to an Army Air Corps motion picture unit in Culver City, Calif. He made 400 training films, appeared opposite Joan Leslie in *This Is the Army* (1943) and, before being discharged in late 1945, was promoted, which yielded a valuable portfolio of photographs depicting Captain Reagan in uniform.

He stood out among his colleagues in

other ways, too. Moralistic, sober and monogamous in Sodom, he was seen by some as a bore. Brazen Bette Davis thought him "a silly boy." Hollywood's liberal intellectuals considered him and his Midwestern attitudes shallow, while the town's revelers couldn't understand his abiding passion for politics. This was chiefly manifested, at the time, in the active role he played with the Screen Actors Guild. He had served on the board as early as 1941, and in 1947 he succeeded Robert Montgomery as president. In the turbulent Red Scare period, when Congress was weeding out Hollywood's

communists, Reagan was a strong, stalwart leader. In '47 he told the House Un-American Activities Committee that, while communism was no doubt an evil, any blacklisting or censorship of his fellow actors was unwarranted. What one commentator called "a fine statement of civil-libertarian principles" got him branded a dangerous liberal by others. As a union activist, Reagan at one point received death threats and began packing a pistol for protection. Even as his acting career was stalled (one pedestrian film after another, a stream of mild second-banana parts, a highlight of sorts being his

Reagan was a seven-term president of the Screen Actors Guild in the 1940s and '50s. In October 1946 (above), Jane Wyman, Henry Fonda, Reagan, Boris Karloff and Gene Kelly discussed crossing a picket line at an emergency meeting of the union. The following October, Reagan testified before the House Un-American Activities Committee (opposite). In 1947 he was finally fitted for contact lenses, and rarely again appeared in public wearing glasses.

He made some good pictures—really! *Bedtime for Bonzo* **(1951, left) was an amiable screwball comedy. In 1950's poignant** *The Hasty Heart* **(above), Reagan played opposite Patricia Neal. In** *The Winning Team* **(1952, right), he was winning as Grover Cleveland Alexander.**

famous performance opposite Bonzo), Reagan became obsessed with his real-world role as a political figure.

Jane Wyman sued for divorce in 1948, complaining among other things that her husband "talked about politics at every meal." Reagan put on a brave face, joking publicly about the film for which Wyman won her '48 Oscar: "I think I'll name *Johnny Belinda* as the co-respondent." In fact, he was devastated. He was seen at parties with tears in his eyes. He descended into "a lonely inner world," he admitted much later. "My loneliness was not from being unloved, but rather from not loving . . . Real loneliness is not missing anyone at all."

Actors William Holden and Brenda Marshall (his wife) attended Ron and Nancy at their wedding on March 4, 1952. The newlyweds honeymooned in Phoenix (above). In the fall of '52, Patti Reagan was born, and Dad campaigned as a Democrat for Eisenhower.

In the early '50s a pretty, big-eyed actress named Nancy Davis heard that her name had been attached to left-wing groups then under investigation. Nancy, from a well-to-do, conservative background in Chicago, went to SAG for help in clearing her name. Her hero at the union, Ronald Reagan, allowed her to help him in turn. "Although he loves people, he often seems remote, and he doesn't let anybody get too close," Nancy wrote years later. "There's a wall around him. He lets me come closer than anyone else, but there are times when even I feel that barrier."

Presidents in the Movies

Ronald Reagan was our only actor-President, but there were lots of other actors who portrayed the President. Here are examples from the intersection of Sunset Boulevard and Pennsylvania Avenue.

Anthony Hopkins as Richard Nixon
In 1995 director Oliver Stone, who had made revisionist history with *JFK,* struck again with *Nixon.* He cast an Englishman in the title role.

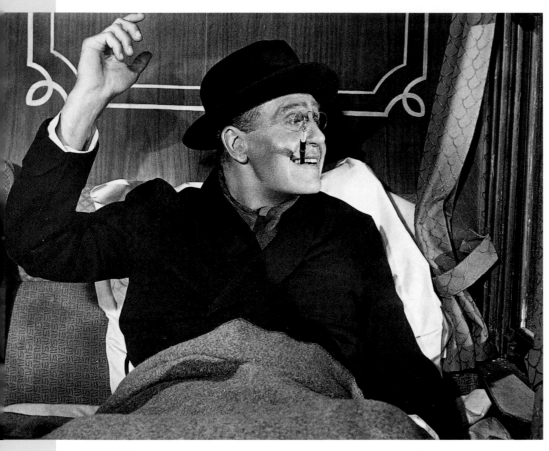

Ralph Bellamy as Franklin D. Roosevelt
In 1960, Bellamy reprised his Broadway triumph in the film version of Dore Schary's play *Sunrise at Campobello.*

Nick Nolte as Thomas Jefferson
The U.S. ambassador fell for artist Maria Cosway (played by Greta Scacchi), according to 1995's *Jefferson in Paris.*

Charlton Heston as Andrew Jackson
In 1953's *The President's Lady,* Heston was cast as Tennessee's favorite son. He would again play his Old Hickory five years later in *The Buccaneer.*

Henry Fonda
as Abraham Lincoln

The critic Pauline Kael considered 1939's *Young Mr. Lincoln,* about an Illinois country lawyer, "one of [director] John Ford's most memorable films."

Cliff Robertson as
John F. Kennedy

In 1963, months before JFK was assassinated, a movie depicting his World War II heroism was released. Kennedy himself had picked Robertson for the lead in *PT 109.*

John Travolta as "Jack Stanton"

Emma Thompson and Travolta were not Hillary and Bill Clinton—sure—in 1998's *Primary Colors,* based on the book by Anonymous, not Joe Klein.

Alexander Knox
as Woodrow Wilson

The character actor Knox was superb in the 1944 biopic *Wilson;* he garnered one of the film's 11 Oscar nominations. *Wilson* took home six statuettes.

A Time of Transition

Ronald Reagan, the movie star, was on his first tour as General Electric's front man/pitchman/booster/glad-hander/communicator. The plan was for Reagan, the new host of the television show *General Electric Theater,* to visit 139 plants across the country, bucking up 250,000 employees. He would listen to their concerns and share his thoughts. This mightn't have been everyone's idea of a good time, but it sure was Reagan's.

Kicking off the tour at the giant turbine plant in Schenectady, N.Y., he had a ball. He signed hundreds of autographs, had his back slapped by a hundred guys, sent a hundred gals swooning.

As the night wound down, a request came via Reagan's speechwriter Earl Dunckel. There was a convention of high school teachers in town, and their speaker had taken ill. Could Mr. Reagan take his place? "Dunk, let's give it a try," he replied.

The next day, Ronald Reagan took flight on education, offering everything he remembered—facts, fancies, theories. Four thousand teachers sat rapt, then leapt to their feet and cheered. The thunderous applause lasted 10 minutes. Earl Dunckel, off to the side, shook his head in wonder.

Reagan was 43 and a fading star when he signed to host General Electric's weekly anthology in 1954. His association with the company not only allowed him to perfect meet-and-greet skills that would serve him immensely well, it also kept him before the public at large: *General Electric Theater* was one of TV's top-rated shows during the late '50s.

Greetings from Las Vegas

Ronald Reagan, joyous in his new marriage, was miserable as an actor. Warner Bros. had dumped him and offers were few. What films he did land were B-minus. "*Tropic Zone* and *Law and Order* both gave me that I-don't-want-to-go-out-in-the-lobby feeling," he recalled. On occasion, he turned down work because he felt victimized by the 91 percent tax bracket; he became a crusader against an "evil" tax system that soaked the rich—including glamorous Hollywood movie stars. Reagan eventually went into debt, in part because the Internal Revenue Service made him a poster boy for his new issue by smacking him with a back-taxes assessment.

Needing money, Reagan accepted a two-week gig in 1954 as emcee at a two-bit Vegas nightclub in a hotel chillingly

Well, the Coconut Grove doesn't come cheap. Reagan played Vegas in 1954 (above) for the money, and shilled for Rheingold beer in 1955 (below). He and Nancy enjoyed a splendid evening at L.A.'s chichi Grove in '57 (opposite).

MPTV

Double duty: Hosting G.E.'s show (left) and meeting the rank and file. The plant tours sharpened Reagan's political skills as well as his ideas. At one factory he shook 2,000 hands, at another he signed 10,000 photos. At Appliance Park in Louisville, Ky., Reagan walked 46 miles of assembly line (or so he claimed). He returned after dark and walked the night shift.

named the Last Frontier. Taking the stage, he said, "When it was announced I was going to do a floor show, someone said, 'What's he going to do?' That's a very good question—I wish I had a very good answer—so does the fellow who asked me—he runs this place." (Ra-ta-*boom!*)

"It was a great experience," Reagan said later, finding that silver lining. "But two weeks were enough."

What next? Well, for a Hollywood actor in 1953 there was one venue just as dicey as a Vegas dive, and that was TV. Jungle law said if you opted for the small box, you were through on the big screen. But Reagan could refuse no longer. The offer he accepted—to host a series of dramas sponsored by G.E. at an annual salary of $125,000—was a good, respectable one. (The biggest benefits of this deal wouldn't be realized for another decade.)

Reagan was not hired merely to be host of, and occasional actor in, the tele-

plays. As roving ambassador in the G.E. universe, he sought to explain management to labor. This marked a third stage in his relationship with workers. The son of a working stiff, he had nevertheless derided the Screen Actors Guild when he got to Hollywood. Then, coaxed by a fellow actor, he had become a union stalwart. Now he was a missionary for a notoriously antiunion company. "Boulwarism," after G.E.'s fierce vice president Lemuel Boulware, was a dread term to labor lawyers, but Reagan was management's gung ho foot soldier among G.E.'s employees. That he was able to develop not only a constituency but also a cult among the working class is yet more evidence of the man's innate charisma and nonpareil salesmanship.

As Reagan was evolving into a different kind of public figure, his politics were shifting too. It wasn't just taxes and Boulwarism, it was everything. His problems

with the IRS led to other conservative impulses: antiwelfare, anti-big-government. With each passing day, the hard times of Dixon receded further, and the influence of years among the privileged gained purchase. And then there was the Nancy factor. Whereas Jane Wyman had grown so weary of Reagan's political obsessions that she showed him the door, Nancy, imbued with conservative values, listened intently to her husband's speeches. As he drifted right, she assured him it was the right way to drift.

Reagan often said that changing parties was as hard as changing religions—explanation for staying a Democrat so

Hellcats of the Navy **(1957, opposite) was Reagan and Davis's only feature together and would have been Reagan's last film except that the prospective television drama** *The Killers* **(above, featuring Angie Dickinson) was deemed too violent for TV and was released in theaters in 1964. In 1954, Reagan was targeted by James Dean on** *G.E. Theater* **(right).**

long. But finally there was no room in a party dominated by Kennedyism and heading toward LBJ's Great Society.

He was giving a speech near his home in Pacific Palisades in 1962. The themes were reflective of his conservative views, and in the middle of his talk one woman in the audience couldn't take it anymore.

"Mr. Reagan!" she shouted, gaining her feet. "I have a question. Have you registered as a Republican yet?"

"Well, no, but I intend to."

The woman stormed the stage. "I'm a registrar," she said, and she thrust a form at him. He signed, and that was that: Ronald Reagan, Republican.

The Reagans, along with actor Don DeFore (to Nancy's right)—as well as Andy Devine, John Wayne, Jane Russell, Linda Darnell and other stars—got a charge out of the rabid, placard-carrying audience at an anticommunism rally at the Hollywood Bowl in 1961.

The Great Communicators

By the time Ronald Reagan made the nickname his own, there had already been several Presidents who had a similarly uncanny ability to connect with the American people.

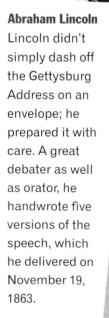

Abraham Lincoln
Lincoln didn't simply dash off the Gettysburg Address on an envelope; he prepared it with care. A great debater as well as orator, he handwrote five versions of the speech, which he delivered on November 19, 1863.

Theodore Roosevelt
T.R.'s dynamism was heroic—one time, literally so. Challenging for the White House in 1912, he was shot by a would-be assassin. He gave his speech, then sought a doctor.

Executive Mansion,

*Washington, _____, 186_*

Four score and seven years ago our fathers brought forth, upon this continent, a new nation, conceived in liberty, and dedicated to the proposition that "all men are created equal"

Now we are engaged in a great civil war, testing whether that nation, or any nation so conceived, and so dedicated, can long endure. We are met on a great battle field of that war. We have come to dedicate a portion of it, as a final resting place for those who died here, that the nation might live. This we may, in all propriety do. But, in a larger sense, we can not dedicate—we can not consecrate—we can not hallow, this ground— The brave men, living and dead, who struggled here, have hallowed it, far above our poor power to add or det...

CLOCKWISE FROM TOP LEFT: BROWN BROTHERS; FPG; UPI/CORBIS-BETTMANN; PAUL SCHUTZER, CORBIS-BETTMANN; LIBRARY OF CONGRESS

Franklin D. Roosevelt

From 1933 through 1944, FDR gave 30 Fireside Chats. For his New Deal he asked a "spirit of mutual confidence and mutual encouragement," which is just what the radio chats fostered.

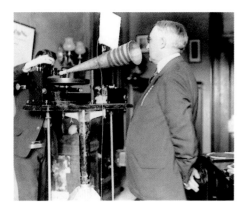

Warren G. Harding

By the time Harding took office in 1921, Marconi and Edison had changed the ways a President could communicate. He could take to the airwaves, or wax his eloquence.

John F. Kennedy and Richard Nixon

When JFK bested Nixon in four debates during the '60 campaign, another new criterion was established. A great communicator now had to be not only forceful and eloquent but telegenic. Great hair helped, as Kennedy and Reagan learned.

Governor Reagan

He stood in a light blue suit that picked up his light blue eyes; his left hand was stuck deep into his pants pocket. He gestured with his right hand, moving it around, touching the podium with his fingertips. About to deliver a punch line, he touched his right eyebrow. The joke went over well. The audience, tipped it was coming, had grown anxious, then had responded with a big laugh.

He was asked a question. He cocked his head to the right, not unlike a fighter sidestepping a jab. "Well." He said it with emphasis—"Weellll"—while wearing an easy smile. Then he answered.

One day in the '60s, when young people were at the barricades on college campuses across the country, the question to the governor was this: "Aren't these kids just rebelling against the principles and standards we were raised on and which we've been trying to pass on to them?"

"Perhaps," Reagan said, "young people aren't rebelling against our standards. Perhaps they're rebelling because they don't think we are living by the standards we've tried to teach them."

The hall was silent for a moment, then trembled, then erupted. He did know how to work a crowd.

REPUBLICAN
NATIONAL
CONVENTION
1968

At the '64 Republican convention (opposite), Ronald Reagan, aging movie star, worked the room, expressing support for Barry Goldwater. That support reached a national TV audience on October 27 when Reagan delivered his famous speech A Time for Choosing (left). "We can preserve for our children this last, best hope of man on earth," said the new political star.

Ronald Reagan became very good at disclaiming. In the early 1960s, friends were urging the former union chief to consider political office. He'd smile and say thank you and then, "Well, ahh, no, I don't think so." In 1961 the California state Republican chairman said at a news conference that the party's best chances to wrest the governorship in 1962 lay with Richard Nixon and that strong-spoken actor fellow, Ronald Reagan (who wasn't yet a Republican). Replied Reagan: "It would represent too much of a change in my way of living and what I'm trying to do." As if to emphasize, when his contract with G.E. expired, Reagan let it be known to Hollywood friends that he would like to resuscitate his movie career. He narrated *The Young Doctors* in 1961, and when

The Killers metamorphosed from a television production to a feature film, he was back on the big screen. But that would be the end of the movie career: A man with Reagan's political inclinations and personal ambition could disclaim only so long.

In 1965, Reagan, now visible primarily as the host of another TV anthology, the oater *Death Valley Days,* was asked by Republican politicos to be cochairman of the California Citizens for Goldwater committee, an effort to elect conservative Arizona Sen. Barry Goldwater President. Reagan, a true believer in Goldwater conservatism, said sure, this I can do. He traveled the state giving "The Speech," which was basically a harangue against big government and the welfare system. In late summer, party bosses again came to Reagan with a proposition: If they paid for

some national TV time, would Reagan give a speech boosting Barry? Reagan said sure, this I can do.

A Time for Choosing was "The Speech" writ much, much larger. It, and the speaker, were magnificent, and when Reagan summed up with "You and I have a rendezvous with destiny," Joe Sixpack turned from the tube and said to the missus, "Hey, why ain't Ronnie running?"

But Ronnie wasn't, and Barry got whomped—one of the worst thrashings in presidential election history.

Reagan emerged from the debacle of 1964 not only unscathed but a political star. His magnetic delivery of A Time for Choosing had drawn a thousand letters of congratulation and invitation, as well as a million dollars to Republican coffers. Reagan's suitors would press their suit harder this time. They came to his

In 1965, Bill Ray visited Pacific Palisades and took these rarely seen pictures for LIFE. By then, Reagan's family was complete. Maureen and Michael were grown; Nancy and Ronald's daughter Patti, born in 1952, wasn't home, but Ron, born in 1958, was. Reagan is acting here: By his kids' accounts, he was an aloof dad.

house and told him he was the man to beat Pat Brown for governor. "I kept saying no," Reagan remembered later. "I had a good job and a good life, and at 54, the last thing I wanted to do was start a new career."

The political operatives asked Reagan to at least test the waters with a swing around the state. The response to his tour was such that Reagan was compelled to run. The race against Brown, a liberal who was seeking a third term, was vicious. While Reagan was only six years the younger man, he would do impressions on the stump of a doddering Brown (never worrying, certainly, that the issue of a candidate's age might plague him, too, one day). Brown, for his part, kept asking voters if they wanted an actor for governor. The way he sneered "actor," it equated with idiot.

He was ready for the role, expert at pressing the flesh or riding a horse (here in San Jose's Mexican Independence Day parade during the '66 campaign). Herbert Gold called him "a heavenly Pop politician in the paradise of Pop art."

In the early '60s the idea of people like Ronald Reagan being active in politics was, to many, ludicrous. Electing an entertainer to high office was a bridge not to be crossed, just as the election of a Catholic President was an impossibility before John F. Kennedy. The idea that actors do nothing but pretend was hammered home even by some of Reagan's showbiz brethren, including an old liberal-leaning compadre from SAG. "I've

played many roles before the camera," Gene Kelly said in a political commercial. "I know I could *play* the role of a governor but that I could never really sit in his chair and make decisions affecting the education of millions of children."

As it happened, Californians like their actors, or at least they liked this actor, plenty. Reagan beat Brown by nearly a million votes; it was a landslide of LBJ proportions. Overnight he was the leader of the country's most populous state and, also, the national leader of the conservative movement.

The very moment Reagan achieved the State House he started disclaiming again—"Well, ahh, no, I don't think so"— about designs on the White House.

Reagan won big in '66 (left), then got down to business with aides (above, from left) Lyn Nofziger, Tom Reed and Art Van Court. As governor, Reagan had to overcome his fear of flying. LIFE photographer John Loengard said of the photo opposite: "He was this happy because he was back on the ground."

FRED KAPLAN

RALPH CRANE

Some well-scrubbed young people carried his posters, others picked a fight. In February 1967 in Sacramento (left), he confronted University of California students demonstrating at the capitol against budget cuts and the introduction of tuition.

Meanwhile, he set about building a reputation as a strong, innovative governor. Some things might have been anticipated—his opposition to handgun control, his support of capital punishment and, in his first term, his tough response to the People's Park takeover at the University of California at Berkeley, which saw the National Guard patrolling city streets for a full 17 days. But other initiatives remain surprising all these years later. He signed a liberalized abortion law; his much-lauded welfare reforms included a 41 percent increase for the neediest; he put on the books the toughest water-quality standards in the country; he signed several measures banning discrimination against women and one that protected rape victims from public questioning about their sex lives. Reagan's government commissions were multicultural—

he appointed more minorities than had any previous California governor—and he saw to it that many bilingual services were added for Spanish-speaking citizens (even as he fought Cesar Chavez's efforts to unionize migrant farmworkers). In 1972 he told Equal Rights Amendment lobbyists that they had his "full support." As President, Ronald Reagan would flip on several of these issues, but during eight years as California's governor he was building a record that would make it easy—enticing, even—for those who would come to be known as Reagan Democrats to join him in his tent.

Among the many people dismayed by

Richard Nixon's resignation was Ronald Reagan, and he had personal reasons. The rise of Gerald Ford to the presidency put a crimp in Reagan's designs on the 1976 Republican nomination. He made a charge anyway, and it was a strong one. Ford remembered later: "Some of my closest advisers . . . had been warning me for months to prepare for a difficult challenge from Ronald Reagan. I hadn't taken those warnings seriously because I didn't take Reagan seriously." Pat Brown had made the same mistake.

Ford survived Reagan but lost to Jimmy Carter. Reagan survived 1976 with a million dollars left over, and he used this

The derision aimed at Reagan "the actor" engendered a campaign backlash and drew cronies such as Bob Hope, John Wayne, Dean Martin and Frank Sinatra to the fore. Sinatra became a particular friend of the Reagans (opposite) and would be a frequent White House guest.

to launch, in January 1977, his Citizens for the Republic political action committee. Carter hadn't been inaugurated yet, but the 1980 presidential race had already begun. There was no more disclaiming; Ronald Reagan needed no more convincing. He was ready for his rendezvous with destiny.

Prominent First Ladies

Some Presidents' wives were all but invisible. Some others, like Nancy Reagan, held the public eye. And a few even held real power.

Edith Wilson
Some were powers behind the throne. Was Woodrow Wilson's wife the power *on* the throne? Some say she was in 1919 and '20 after first a breakdown, then a stroke, left the President severely diminished. The smart, strong Mrs. Wilson was an able deputy.

Dolley Madison
During a British attack in 1814, Dolley grabbed the Declaration of Independence, the Constitution and a portrait of George Washington.

Abigail Adams
Her husband, John, the second President, called her Partner. She groomed their son John Quincy to follow Dad's path.

Harriet Lane
Her uncle, the bachelor James Buchanan, leaned on her for hostessing in 1857, and the 26-year-old became D.C.'s darling.

Caroline Harrison
Benjamin's wife was the "best housekeeper the White House has ever known"—sumptuous praise in the Gilded Age.

Florence Harding

Warren was pudding next to the formidable Flossie. "Well," she said after the 1920 election, "I have got you the presidency; what are you going to do with it?"

Jacqueline Kennedy

JFK's wife presided as queen of Camelot, imbuing the White House with glamour and style while hosting new kinds of guests, like French man of letters André Malraux (above).

Eleanor Roosevelt

Feminist, diplomat, crusader: FDR's wife proved that the First Lady could be an overt—and effective—political being.

Hillary Clinton

An official aide to, and defender of, her husband, she began her own bid for public office while still First Lady.

President Reagan

One day in 1982, as Ronald Reagan was in the White House reading *The Washington Post,* he came across a disturbing item. A black family, the Butlers of College Park, Md., had been harassed. A cross had been burned on their lawn.

This was 1982, not 1962, and Ronald Reagan was now President of the United States, not a B-list actor hanging out by the pool in Pacific Palisades. He could do something about this.

As leader of the Free World he was a busy man, but he ordered his schedule cleared and summoned the motorcade—the whole sirens-blaring motorcade. In College Park, the presidential limo pulled up curbside; Ron and Nancy Reagan got out and crossed the Butlers' small lawn. "They were a nice couple with a four-year-old daughter and a grandma, a most gracious lady, living with them," Reagan said. "Their home was comfortably and tastefully furnished. We enjoyed our visit, and when it was time to leave they saw us to our car." Reagan made a bit of a show in bidding farewell, waving to neighbors who had gathered.

"Needless to say," he recalled with satisfaction, "this fine family had no further harassment."

"There is, in America, a greatness and a tremendous heritage of idealism, which is a reservoir of strength and goodness. It is ours if we will but tap it. And because of this—because that greatness is there—there is need in America today for a reaffirmation of that goodness and a re-formation of our greatness."—Ronald Reagan, 1981. The opinion was an honest one, for there was in him a tremendous heritage of idealism, a reservoir of strength and goodness.

He once said that "nothing thrilled me more than looking up at a windblown flag while listening to a choir sing 'The Battle Hymn of the Republic,' my favorite song." From 1981 through '88, he would have many an opportunity to experience that thrill from a special vantage point. But first he had to win the role.

In 1980, Ronald Reagan, former actor and ex-governor, knew something about winning a role. He knew about forceful gestures and seizing the moment. For example, George Bush had beaten him in the Iowa caucuses and was giving him trouble in the polls on the eve of the New Hampshire primary, making hay with assaults on Reagan's "voodoo economics." But at a debate in Nashua, Reagan refused to be cut off, declaring, "I paid for this microphone!" Indeed, Reagan's campaign may have paid for the hall, and certainly there were aspects of Reagan's "trickle-down" economic plan that may have looked like voodoo, at least hoodoo—

Even before he said he was running, he was running; even when he was resting, he was running. He had a huge war chest left over from 1976 (opposite, campaigning in Tampico, Ill., in front of the building in which he was born). With the money, he formed his political committee, then retired to plot his strategy (above, at his California ranch).

At the Kentucky Derby in 1980, the candidate tried out the winner's circle. He said he was a "citizen politician" who was running on behalf of his fellow citizens. He asked the electorate that summer: "If not us, then who? If not now, when?"

suddenly, none of it mattered. Bush was a wimp, Reagan was a warrior, and in flinty New Hampshire, where the state motto is Live Free or Die, warriors crush wimps every time. Reagan thrashed Bush in the primary, 51 percent to 22, and cruised to his party's nomination. Sixty-nine years old, with his last, best chance to be President, he was playing to win.

If George Bush, a bona fide World War II hero, could be made to look weak by Ronald Reagan, then mild-mannered Jimmy Carter could be made to look anemic. Carter's economic program had failed miserably, and he had, only shortly before the national campaign began, seemed to castigate his countrymen for a sullen state of affairs in America, citing "a crisis of confidence . . . that strikes at the very heart and soul and spirit of our national will." Reagan said there was no spiritual crisis that would not be cured by a switch in tenancy at 1600 Pennsylvania Avenue: "I find no national malaise, I find nothing wrong with the American people." Joe Sixpack turned to the missus and said, "Is Jimmy trying to blame us for this hostage thing? I'm voting for Ronnie."

In January 1979, Iranian zealots had forced the shah to leave; in November they had taken 52 American hostages—diplomatic emissaries of the "Great Satan." As the days of the hostage crisis

were tallied by news anchors, respect for Jimmy Carter evaporated drop by drop. Reagan finished him off in the "There you go again" debate of October 28 when he summed up for the American people thusly: "Are you better off than you were four years ago? . . . Is America as respected throughout the world as it was?"

Had the mullahs' prisoners been released in 1980, then in all probability Carter would have prevailed. As it was,

Reagan won the election by 10 percentage points, Republicans took control of the Senate, Democrats lost 31 seats in the House, and on January 20, 1981, Americans watched split-screen coverage of Ronald Wilson Reagan being sworn in as the 40th President while a 444-day nightmare ended with the release of the hostages, who flew from Tehran 28 minutes after Reagan took his oath.

Reagan strove to appear fresh and dif-

"This country doesn't have to be in the shape that it is in." So spoke the challenger in his October 1980 debate with Carter. As the candidates kissed their wives (above), Carter's campaign was crashing and Reagan's, opposite, soaring.

On January 20, 1981, the Reagans took over the White House. The President recalled his father's old shoe business when he said, "I'm back living above the store again." Shortly after his swearing-in by Chief Justice Warren Burger, he joked, "It's been a very wonderful day. I guess I can go back to California, can't I?"

ferent. The first President inaugurated on the West Front of the Capitol, with its sweeping view of the great monuments, he pledged in his address "an era of national renewal." His dashing performance over the next several days was beyond boffo. The inauguration, a three-day, $8 million bash—which kicked off with an $800,000 fireworks display, featured nine balls and starred A-list talent from Johnny Carson to Frank Sinatra—was a smash; Gary Wills called it "Hollywood on the Potomac." The release of the hostages had spurred a national euphoria, and it seemed as if every citizen from Portland to Portland was dancing at the party. The glamour was all the more pronounced for its stark contrast with the cornpone image of the Carter White House. It was as if Ron and Nancy were sweeping out any straw left behind by the hillbillies from Georgia, proclaiming a second coming of Camelot. (In fact, it was almost precisely like that: The Reagans reinstated the White House trumpeters, banished by the Carters; a color guard to precede the presidential

The Reagans and
friends, including
Frank Sinatra, danced
the night away.
The photo above
displeased Michael
Deaver, who felt
Sinatra's alleged
mob links made
him too hot for the
White House.

family's entrance was restored as well.)

Nancy, a self-proclaimed "frustrated interior decorator," raised nearly a million dollars among rich friends to help her spiff up the mansion. She accepted from a private donor a 220-place setting of china, the first new china in the White House in nearly two decades. She presided at elaborate gourmet dinners. *The Wall Street Journal* reported, "In the early days, the Carters didn't give their guests anything to drink. Then they added table wine . . . But now, with the Reagans, booze is back."

After the first flush of excitement wore off, critics began disapproving of such splendor, saying it was offensive at a time of widespread economic misery. A hot-selling postcard in 1981 showed "Queen Nancy" in a crown, and a reporter wrote that she "was using her position to improve the quality of life for those in the White House." Mrs. Reagan was hurt by the broadsides but did nothing to change her ways. Her disapproval rating in the first term climbed to the highest of any modern First Lady.

Ronald Reagan said once, "I remember John Kennedy saying that when he came into office, the thing that surprised him the most was to find that things were just as bad as he'd been saying they were. In my case, the biggest surprise was find-

The puritans had been routed, prohibition was over, the booze was back. On his first workday, Reagan was all business in the Oval Office (above). But not long after, at a White House party in honor of Walter Cronkite's retirement from CBS, a hearty toast was enjoyed by the President, the honoree and Vice President Bush (second from right), among others.

ing out that they were even worse." He meant the economy. "I arrived in the White House as the country was experiencing what many called its greatest economic emergency since the Depression . . . My advisers and I had begun working on a recovery plan the first day after the election. The morning after Inauguration Day, we began implementing the plan. Its basis was tax reform."

Whether Reagan's supply-side economic recovery program, which argued that tax cuts all the way up the economic ladder (big business included) would stimulate prosperity all the way down, was a disaster for the poor during the 1980s, or whether it was the bedrock on which the fantastic growth of the 1990s was built, would prove a debate never to be settled.

Reagan cast his attention unwaveringly upon the economic plan during his first weeks in office, and it was a topic he would concentrate on in his speech at the Washington Hilton to the Construction Trades Council on March 30. He put on a new blue suit that morning and a favorite old wristwatch that Nancy had given him. He felt good, but the speech

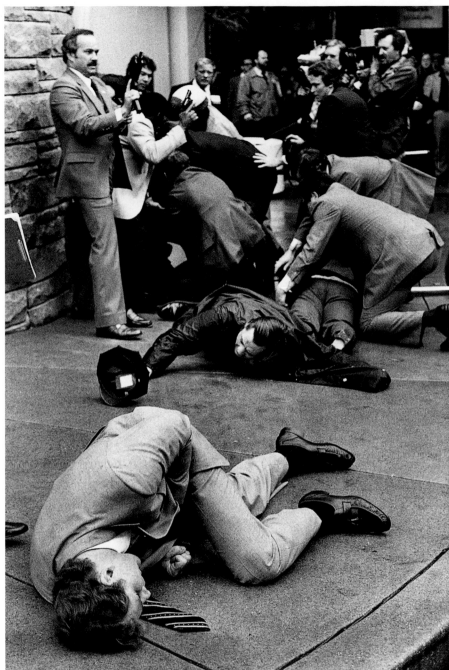

March 30, 1981: As Secret Service agent Parr (behind Reagan) pushed the President into the limo, Parr's colleague Timothy J. McCarthy was wounded (above, foreground; in background, other agents cover fallen press secretary Brady, who is facedown). Hinckley is seized (right). At the hospital, Reagan asked, "Does anybody know what that guy's beef was?" Later, while Hinckley's mental illness didn't satisfy those who wanted his scalp, it was enough for Reagan: "He wasn't thinking on all cylinders."

Remedies for the healing President came in all shapes and sizes. A distraught Nancy arrived at the hospital bearing Ron's beloved jelly beans. The White House staff posed for a huge get-well card and sent copies to the four men wounded by Hinckley.

was only politely received. "I think most of the audience were Democrats," he said.

He left the hotel through a side entrance and passed the ever-present photographers. He was about to climb into the limo when he heard something—"just a small fluttering sound, *pop, pop, pop*"—to his left. He turned and said, "What the hell's that?" Secret Serviceman Jerry Parr knew what it was and threw Reagan into the car. "I landed on my face atop the armrest across the backseat and Jerry jumped on top of me," Reagan remembered. "When he landed, I felt a pain in my upper back that was unbelievable." He yelled for Parr to get off him, thinking the agent had broken one of his ribs. "The White House!" Parr shouted, and the car sped off. Reagan tried to sit up. He coughed. That was when he saw "the palm of my hand was

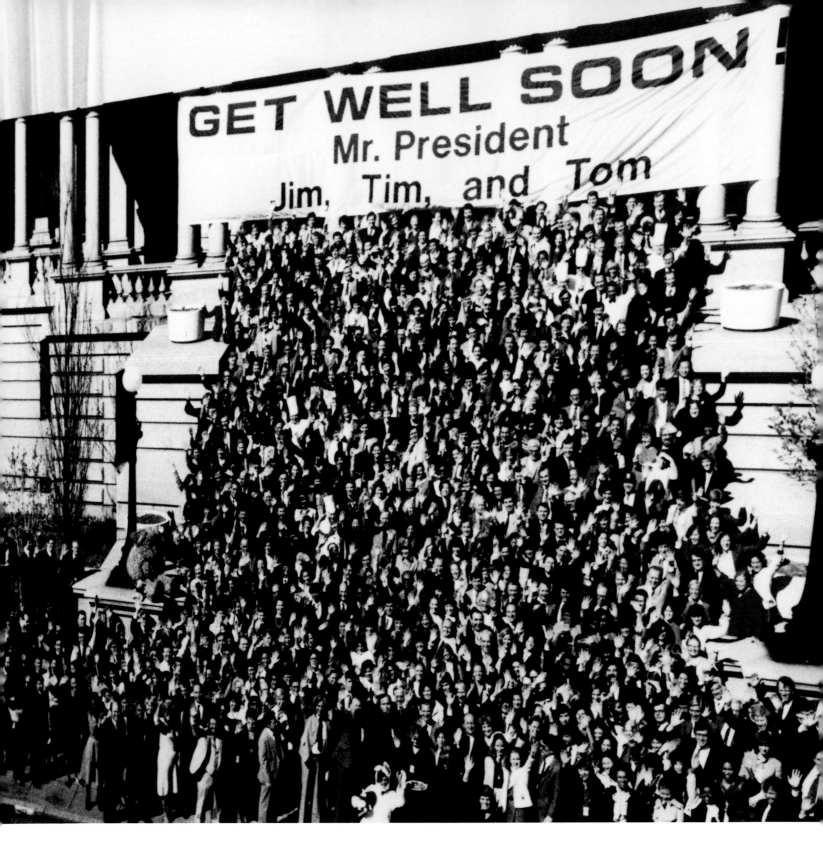

GET WELL SOON!
Mr. President
Jim, Tim, and Tom

brimming with extremely red, frothy blood." Parr saw the hand too, and told the driver to head for George Washington University Hospital instead.

Assaults on U.S. Presidents have been made by men and women, the politically motivated and the frustrated, sane men and madmen. And what was John W. Hinckley Jr.? He was a 25-year-old son of a Denver oil executive. He was a man who, on March 30, was packing a .22-caliber pistol, despite the fact that he had been arrested on a concealed weapons charge in Nashville a few months earlier. He was mentally ill. He had been in treatment before and at one point had developed an obsession with Jodie Foster after seeing her in *Taxi Driver*. In that film, a character played by Robert De Niro tries to assassinate a senator in hopes of attracting a woman's attention.

On August 13, 1981, he signed his tax bill on a foggy day at Rancho del Cielo. "I've been told that some members of Congress disagree with my tax-cut proposal," he had said in a speech. "Well, you know it's been said that taxation is the art of plucking the feathers without killing the bird. It's time they realized the bird doesn't have any feathers left."

Hinckley squeezed off six shots outside the Hilton. Press secretary James S. Brady was hit in the head and would be paralyzed for life. A police officer and a Secret Service agent also were wounded. The bullet that caught Reagan ricocheted off the limo, then bounced off a rib and lodged in his lung, an inch from his heart.

The nation did not know, at the time, just how critical the President's condition was—and this had everything to do with the brave, graceful manner with which Reagan confronted the situation. He tried to walk into the hospital under his own power until his knees buckled. Lying on the gurney, he told one surgeon, "I hope you're a Republican," to which the loyal Democrat replied, "Today, Mr. President, we're all Republicans." When Nancy arrived at her husband's bedside, he used a line from the boxer Jack Dempsey: "Honey, I forgot to duck."

Reagan's recovery from his brush with death was remarkably quick, and though not fully healed, he left the hospital 12 days after entering. During that time his popularity had soared to new heights, and now aides James Baker and Michael Deaver persuaded him to use this to advantage in selling his economic plan. Less than a month after the attack by Hinckley, who was meantime heading to a psychiatric facility, Reagan lectured

Michael Deaver once suggested that Reagan spend less time at Rancho del Cielo. The boss looked his aide in the eye and said he could question anything except the visits to the ranch.

Congress on the wisdom of supply-side thinking. The address helped shore up the bipartisan coalition Reagan needed for this and other legislation. Also, with the assassination attempt he took on the armor that would lead to what Deaver termed his Teflon presidency. For seven more years, critics could assail Reaganomics or Iran-Contra all they chose, but if they attacked the man himself, a figure beloved by his countrymen, they did so at their considerable peril.

While there was this arguably positive fallout from Hinckley's assault—an upsurge in devotion, a Teflon coating—

there were curious aftereffects as well. Reagan wrote in his diary, "Whatever happens now I owe my life to God and will try to serve Him in every way I can," but Nancy turned ever more fervently to astrology to help her guide the family. It was rumored that the precise timing of Reagan's inauguration ceremony as governor had been dictated by the planets, and now Nancy insisted that the President's schedule be subject to the influence of her stargazers. Reagan's wife grew more protective of him, and so did his staff, the Secret Service, everyone. This led not only to frustrating episodes on airport tarmacs—Reagan cupping a hand to his ear, indicating to reporters who were a football field away that he couldn't hear them—but also to a gradual disengagement on the part of the Chief Executive.

Reagan, while an impenetrable man with few intimate relationships, had always been a gregarious, handshaking public figure, eager to greet a starstruck fan of *Kings Row,* an assembly-line worker at a G.E. plant or a Democrat primed for conversion. Now no such interaction was possible. He was walled off, and it sapped his spirit. In retrospect, it seems clear that Reagan more purely enjoyed the first nine weeks of his presidency than he did the next seven years, 10 months.

But he served out all that time, the first President since Eisenhower to finish two terms. And an eventful two terms they were. By the end of 1981 he had signed the biggest tax cut in history (25 percent over three years) as well as a budget that was $44.3 billion less than Carter's fiscal '82 budget projection, even

President Reagan, Anglophile, had a close working relationship with Conservative Prime Minister Margaret Thatcher and enjoyed a good laugh or ride with Queen Elizabeth II. "I must admit," Reagan said, "the queen is quite an accomplished horsewoman."

Evenings formal and informal: In 1984 (left) the President caught the news before a state dinner. In 1983 (above) he worked the phones in casual attire. "Most nights after six p.m. [he] would be wearing his nightclothes," said aide Michael Deaver. "The Reagans are probably the biggest pajama fans this side of Hugh Hefner."

though Reagan's contained a $28 billion increase in defense spending. Instead of promoting prosperity, however, Reaganomics ushered the country into a recession. Bankruptcy hit a half-century high, unemployment approached 10 percent (its highest level since the Depression), and an already huge deficit was being padded by the hour. Reagan, shifting gears, asked for the largest tax increase in U.S. history and got it. In 1983 the economy began to revive and unemployment began to drop (it would reach a 15-year low of 5.5 percent by the end of his presidency). Some things got better while some got worse: Domestic prosperity picked up even as the trade deficit quadrupled, making the U.S. the world's largest debtor. The stock market soared to an all-time high just before it crashed. The 508-point fall on October 19, 1987, represented the worst percentage drop in Dow-Jones history. Reaganomics was a roller coaster. The country shut its eyes tight and hoped for the best.

Volatility wasn't restricted to the mar-

On November 4, 1983, at Camp Lejeune, N.C., the Reagans prayed during a memorial service for 241 servicemen killed in the bombing in Beirut and 18 others felled in Grenada. "This is not the happiest of my days as President," said Reagan, "but it's one of my proudest."

kets. Reagan fired 13,000 striking air-traffic controllers in 1981 and called in military personnel to keep the airports open. He elevated conservative Justice William Rehnquist to Chief Justice of the Supreme Court, meanwhile appointing the even more rigid Antonin Scalia to the bench. He tried to install Robert Bork and Douglas H. Ginsburg, but the former was turned down after bitter partisan Senate debate, and the latter withdrew his name after admitting to past marijuana use. (Reagan also named Sandra Day O'Connor to the court early in his tenure, fulfilling a campaign pledge to nominate a woman; later in his second term he promoted the moderate Anthony M. Kennedy after Bork and Ginsburg crashed.) Running for reelection in 1984, Reagan and his vice president and eventual successor, George Bush, beat Walter Mondale and Geraldine Ferraro by the second greatest plurality in a presidential election. Whether Reagan was doing a great, good, adequate or uneven job, Americans loved him all the same.

In January 1986 the space shuttle *Challenger* took off from Cape Canaveral and, to the horror of millions of television viewers, exploded in midair. Aboard was a teacher from New Hampshire, Christa McAuliffe, who had won a contest allowing her to be an astronaut. What would—

At the 1984 Republican national convention in Dallas, the First Lady waved to her husband, the party's nominee-in-waiting, who was watching from a hotel suite with his vice president. The song that played as Nancy waved was "You Are the Sunshine of My Life." In the First Lady's speech, she urged, "Let's make it one more for the Gipper!"

what could?—the Great Communicator do with such a tragedy in his State of the Union address, only hours away?

When faced with specific cases (as opposed to abstractions like "the welfare class"), Ronald Reagan was an innately compassionate man, and there can be little doubt that such affairs as the *Challenger* disaster—or the permanent injury of his friend James Brady, or the killing of 241 Marines when their compound in Beirut was bombed by terrorists in 1983—affected him deeply. An example: Once, a lone-wolf kidnapper threatened to kill his victim unless he got a call from the President. Chief of Staff James Baker was horrified when his boss told him to place the call. Baker talked Reagan out of it and grew increasingly watchful of Reagan's propensity to act on passion, on *feel.*

The *Challenger,* its explosion replayed endlessly on TV monitors and then in the national subconscious, was paradoxically a technological tragedy and an intensely personal one. Reagan would write that McAuliffe's visit to the White House made the disaster "seem even closer and sadder to me." He did the right thing. He canceled the State of the Union address

For a 1985 session with the First Couple, photographer Harry Benson brought a backdrop to the White House (left), then got some memorable up-close-and-personal shots.

and consoled his countrymen. In a moving broadcast, he paraphrased from a sonnet written by an American flier killed in World War II. "We will never forget them," said the President, "nor the last time we saw them this morning as they prepared for their journey and waved goodbye and 'slipped the surly bonds of earth to touch the face of God.'"

Earlier in the day, he and House speaker Tip O'Neill had had acrimonious discussions about Reagan's efforts to cut spending. But O'Neill knew a real thing when he saw one, and said of the President's elegiac speech, "It was a trying day for all Americans, and Ronald Reagan spoke to our highest ideals."

The AIDS epidemic, which erupted

A target once, Reagan, when he wasn't in conference (above, with aides Dennis Thomas, Pat Buchanan, Adm. John Poindexter and David Chew) or isolated in the Oval Office (opposite), moved inside a scrum of Secret Service agents (left).

during his presidency, provides another example of his dealing with an issue only when it was personalized. In the first half of the '80s he thought AIDS was like "measles and . . . would go away." He had nothing against homosexuals, beyond what he called his "old-fashionedness," but many conservatives were telling him to stay away from this issue. Then his friend Rock Hudson, who had been a guest at a recent state dinner, died of complications of AIDS in October 1985.

On July 4, 1986, the Reagans were aboard the USS *Iowa* in New York Harbor to take part in Hollywood producer David Wolper's whiz-bang salute to the century-old Statue of Liberty. The President reviewed 33 vessels from 14 nations, but not the 200 Elvis look-alikes in Wolper's finale.

Shortly afterward, Reagan told the Health and Human Services Department that "one of our highest public-health priorities" was the fight against AIDS.

As for Iran-Contra, the great scandal of the Reagan years: Was it at all personal or wholly political? What did the President know and when did he know it? Was he even paying attention?

As background for an assessment of Iran-Contra, it is useful to look at the Reagan White House's foreign policy in toto. It was defined from Day One as strongly anticommunist and antiterrorist. On March 8, 1983, in a speech in Orlando, Fla., he famously called the Soviet Union an "evil empire" and he backed the Strategic Defense Initiative, an antimissile defense system that would cost billions and was derided by his critics as "Star Wars." Reagan bought Stealth bombers and MX missiles like so many jelly beans, and over a period of six years he shoved a $150 billion defense-budget increase into the evil empire's face.

Then when Moscow blinked and tensions began to thaw, he dealt one-on-one with Mikhail Gorbachev, a man whom, during the Geneva summit of 1985, he had come to know and trust. "I couldn't help but think that something fundamental had changed in the relationship between our countries," Reagan said of

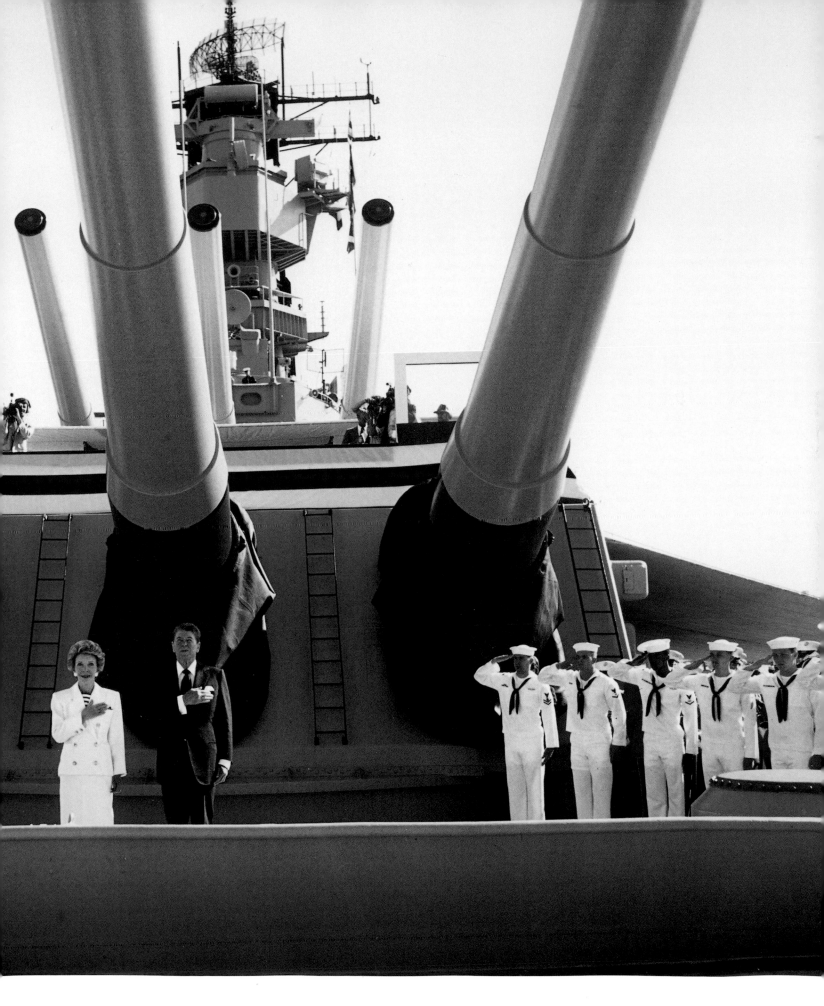

At Geneva (above) and in Washington (left), Gorbachev and Reagan worked to change the world order. Reagan felt a "chemistry" with Gorbachev, "something very close to a friendship."

the Geneva meeting. Reagan and Gorbachev negotiated a reduction in the nuclear stockpile and, eventually, an end to the cold war. Like little kids with a new best pal, each hosted a summit sleepover, and in 1988, Reagan stood at the Berlin Wall and stated: "General Secretary Gorbachev, if you seek peace, if you seek prosperity for the Soviet Union and Eastern Europe, if you seek liberalization, come here to this gate. Mr. Gorbachev, open this gate. Mr. Gorbachev, tear down this wall." He had got to a point in the relationship where his friend—not too strong a word—would listen. The Wall would fall 10 months after Reagan left office.

Back to Iran-Contra: Though Reagan had condemned Iran's holding of hostages in 1980, his administration secretly sold weapons to that country during 1985-86 in exchange for the release of five Americans being held in Lebanon. Millions of dollars from the arms sale were then buried and transferred to the Contras, who were rebel forces in Nicaragua fighting against the leftist Sandinistas—transferred in violation of U.S. policy. Would Ronald Reagan really deal with Tehran? Would he support an effort that flouted Congress? It was clear from the outset that Lt. Col. Oliver North might: Before being convicted of obstructing Congress and other charges (convictions later overturned), he shredded so many documents that the machine jammed twice. But Ronald Reagan?

The President testified that he did not remember authorizing the deal. In a statement to the nation he elaborated somewhat: "The fact of the matter is that

Ron and Nancy (above, on their last day in the White House) bid sentimental farewell. Reagan said that, as President, "you spend a lot of time going by too fast in a car someone else is driving and seeing the people through tinted glass—the parents holding up a child and the wave you saw too late and couldn't return. And so many times I wanted to stop and reach out from behind the glass and connect."

there's nothing I can say that will make the situation right. I was stubborn in my pursuit of a policy that went astray."

No matter what his supporters believed, they were left with dismay. Either he was finally being dishonest after a career of pointing up dishonesty in others; or he was out of touch and freelancers like North were running amok in the White House; or he was fading, losing his memory as sometimes happens with people of 76. Whichever, it was distressing.

Reagan had never been a workaholic Chief Executive, and he found vacations

The torch having been passed, the Bushes were elated, the Reagans resigned. Their relationship had traveled a long road. In 1980, Reagan wondered at his running mate's lack of "spunk" but over eight years grew to like the man immensely and campaigned for him energetically in 1988.

at his 688-acre retreat in the Santa Ynez Mountains near Santa Barbara an important escape. JFK had his Hyannisport, Nixon his San Clemente, and Bush would have Kennebunkport, but perhaps no President ever drew more from his "weekend White House" than Reagan did from Rancho del Cielo. "This is the place where I restore myself," he said.

Everyone in the country knew this, and so when, on January 20, 1989, he handed over the presidency to George Bush and headed west, people felt good for Ronald Reagan. He left the White House with the highest approval rating of any President since Eisenhower.

On that last day, Rex, the Reagans' King Charles spaniel, scooted across the lawn and the President said softly, "There he goes, that's his last walk." Nancy spent the morning wiping away tears. The President's aides, too, were teary-eyed as they surrounded him in the Oval Office. Reagan took out his laminated card that could be used to order a nuclear-missile launch and asked, "Who do I give this to?"

The Notre Dame football team, national champs that year, dropped by and gave Reagan the letter sweater once worn by the real Gipper. His staff gave him a bridle for the hours he would spend riding through the California hills, watching the sun set into the Pacific.

117

Assassinations...

Four United States Presidents were slain while in office, and four others, including Ronald Reagan, were attacked by would-be assassins.

Abraham Lincoln, 1865
Lincoln, attacked once as a President-elect, was killed by Southern sympathizer John Wilkes Booth, an actor, at Ford's Theatre. Booth was shot in the manhunt.

James A. Garfield, 1881
Charles Julius Guiteau, frustrated in his bid for a diplomatic job, shot Garfield on July 2; he lingered for 80 more days. Guiteau was hanged.

John F. Kennedy, 1963
JFK was murdered as his motorcade rolled through Dallas. His assassin, Lee Harvey Oswald, was killed two days later by Jack Ruby.

The Body passing the Treasury. State Funeral of President McKinley
Copyrighted 1901, by William H. Rau.

Sold only by Universal View Co. Philadelphia Pa. Lawrence Kan.

William H. Rau Publisher Philadelphia USA

William McKinley, 1901
At the Pan American Exposition in Buffalo, McKinley was shot by an anarchist named Leon Czolgosz. Even as Washington mourned McKinley (above), New York State moved against Czolgosz. He was electrocuted only 53 days after the attack.

...and Near Assassinations

Gerald Ford, 1975
On September 5, Squeaky Fromme took aim at Ford in Sacramento, and Sara Jane Moore shot at him 17 days later in San Francisco (above). He was unscathed; the women got life.

Andrew Jackson, 1835
Richard Lawrence's assault on Jackson in the Capitol Rotunda was the first attempt on a U.S. President's life. Lawrence, a housepainter, fired at Jackson from six feet but didn't nick him. Found insane, Lawrence was committed for life.

Harry S Truman, 1950
Two Puerto Rican nationalists, Oscar Collazo and Griselio Torresola, attacked Blair House but didn't reach the President. Torresola was killed at the scene. Collazo was wounded (right); he served a life term in prison.

The Legacy

In 1954, Ronald Reagan made a film called *Prisoner of War.* It was about American servicemen who were taken captive during the Korean conflict. While it was far from his best movie, the subject matter resonated for Reagan. It was a patriotic film, of course, and contained tales of quiet bravery, personal heroism. The character he played, Web Sloane, was an intelligence officer who allowed himself to be imprisoned in order to confirm that torture and brainwashing were taking place in Korean camps.

Many times, citing *Prisoner of War,* Reagan would tell his family and others about the horrible treatment that American POWs had received at the hands of the North Koreans. One night late in 1993 the Reagans were having dinner. On this occasion, Ronald's daughter Maureen was telling the war stories, much the same ones her father had told years before. "But now he seemed to be hearing me tell the stories for the first time," Maureen noticed. "Finally he looked at me and said, 'Mermie, I have no recollection of making that movie.'" When his daughter heard this, she suffered what she would call a "click of awareness."

President Reagan, in a 1982 speech to the British Parliament, referred to the Berlin Wall as "that dreadful gray gash across the city . . . a grim symbol of power untamed." In that address he boldly predicted communism would be consigned to "the ash heap of history." By September 12, 1990, when Citizen Reagan took a hammer and chisel to the Wall, the hammer and sickle in Moscow was coming down too.

Ronald Reagan's beloved mother, Nelle, was, in her latter years, what was then called "senile." Her son realized this, of course, and as early as the 1980 campaign, Reagan promised to have his doctors watch him closely for signs of senility, a catchall term for the depredations of old age. By that time most researchers believed that pathological changes in the brain owing to a disease called Alzheimer's were responsible for many of the cases in which old people drift toward dementia. Candidate Reagan said in 1979 that if his doctors found signs that he was fading, he would resign.

He did not, and after serving two terms, Reagan retired to the ranch. He rejoined a private citizenry that was much changed. Reaganomics had started a shift that would continue through the 1990s,

a realignment under which America's rich and powerful grew richer and more powerful, as the disenfranchised sank further. In 1987, 20 percent of U.S. children lived in poverty, representing a 24 percent increase during the Reagan years. In 1989 the wealthiest 40 percent of U.S. families controlled 68 percent of the wealth, while the poorest 40 percent controlled 15 percent: the biggest gap in four decades for which such statistics were kept. Global politics, too, had changed. Most significantly, the cold war was over, the superpowers' nuclear stockpiles were being downsized, and there seemed a sense that Eastern Europe was ready for something truly revolutionary.

Reagan would watch the previously unthinkable happen from Rancho del Cielo. He would marvel as democracy spread west across Europe and in 1990 would himself take a hammer to the wall

Out to pasture at Rancho del Cielo: Reagan and Gorbachev laugh about their gunslinging days (above). Always proper, the former President still dressed for work in his retirement (right).

that had symbolized the Communist–
Free World divide. His legacy to the
world was not a monument that could be
seen but, rather, symbols, barriers and
governments that were vanishing.

He left his nation with an optimism

that was far removed from the malaise
perceived by his predecessor, Jimmy
Carter. Since audiences enjoy gung ho
speeches, early in his retirement Reagan
was able to perform as the embodiment
of positive thinking. He made a bundle

giving speeches; a 1989 trip to Tokyo
brought $2 million for two 20-minute
talks and some handshaking. It was the
ultimate extension of his old G.E. gig.

In the early '90s his appearances
became fewer, his public manner more

disengaged. Other people experienced
that click of awareness.

In 1994 doctors at the Mayo Clinic in
Minnesota diagnosed the former President's illness, and Reagan, in an emotional
handwritten letter, told his countrymen

In Simi Valley in 1991, President George
Bush and predecessors Reagan, Jimmy
Carter, Gerald Ford and Richard Nixon
(left to right, in reverse historical order)
gathered for the dedication of the
Ronald Reagan Presidential Library.

that he had joined the four million of them who suffered from Alzheimer's. The old radio man was, in a sense, signing off: "At the moment I feel just fine. I intend to live the remainder of the years God gives me on this earth doing the things I have always done. I will continue to share life's journey with my beloved Nancy and my family. I plan to enjoy the great outdoors . . . I now begin the journey that will lead me into the sunset of my life. I know that for America there will always be a bright dawn ahead.

"Thank you, my friends. May God always bless you."

And that was the Great Communicator's valedictory. His wife and children became his spokespeople and delivered updates. Nancy, always by his side at the ranch or strolling on the beach, saw her own popularity rise as her evident devotion brought respect from past critics. By humanizing Alzheimer's disease, the chil-

dren helped raise public awareness of a condition that afflicts more than a fifth of Americans after age 85. Michael said candidly in 1995, "He's a vibrant guy who's not so vibrant anymore," and Maureen testified movingly about her father's condition before Congress in 1999.

Eventually, Reagan could no longer enjoy the glories of Rancho del Cielo, and the property was sold in 1998 to Young America's Foundation, an organization dedicated to teaching "future generations of young people about Ronald Reagan's legacy." Ron and Nancy moved permanently to Bel Air.

That's where famous old movie stars live out their lives. It's rarely a retirement spot for sons of the Midwest dust bowl, or even for former U.S. Presidents. But then, nothing was ordinary or predictable about Ronald Reagan's journey from Tampico. It was wholly unpredictable. It was, in every way, extraordinary.

The Reagans enjoyed their early retirement years at the ranch (right) and celebrated Ron's 89th birthday in Bel Air (above). "When our children turn the pages of our lives," President Reagan said in his farewell address, "I hope they'll see that we had a vision to pass forward a nation as nearly perfect as we could."

126

HARRY BENSON

Va te faire foutre Pour
toi va te faire pour
ne m'ait...